ANIMAL POEMS
A to Z

Hayley B. Gowan

Illustrations: Mary Grace Corpus

ISBN: 979-8-218-49469-8 (Paperback Edition)

ISBN: 979-8-218-49470-4 (E-Book Edition)

DEDICATION

These poems, written for my father
Jon Stanton Beazley, Sr.,
were begun in the last years before he died.

AUTHOR'S NOTE

Hoping that my father might repeat the verses with me, they needed to be short as well as entertaining about things he would be interested in.

Keeping them easy to listen to, I decided to do one for an animal of each letter of the alphabet, and the project grew from there.

Only a few, like the first one, D for Dog, flowed without any hesitation. In contrast, most of the rest took weeks to form, and for some, even more time to get the pun or alliteration just right.

Although the initial intent was to keep them simple, the subject matter soon expanded. For instance, the canary poem is about Welsh miners, and to a laughing kookaburra, Oz is slang for Australia.

A

Give two As to the AARDVARK
  The best in his class
Spelling bees were his forte

Thanks to the ABALONE
  London's Pearlie King
A vaudeville act for years

When Portuguese ships saw him
  They'd yell, "Alcatraz!"
Now he's known as ALBATROSS

ALPACAS' wool is so soft
  And so warm, as well
So say the Cuzco ladies

If AMOEBAS need more friends
  Cell division works
Two for one is always good

An ANDEAN PUMA rests
  Chasing prey is hard
Black nights, fierce winds, and deep snow

Like a vast ocean garden
  ANEMONES sway
Their colors pale pink and rose

Black and silvery shadows
  Hints of something there
ANGELFISH dart to and fro

The air's still, the river's dry
  One-ten in the shade
Thirsty ANGUS, wet with sweat

The ANTEATER looks for lunch.
  Somewhere in dead logs
Insects hide 12 inches deep

Their limpid eyes, unblinking
  The ANTELOPES freeze
Unknown scents float in the breeze

What is white in winter time
  And brown in summer?
An Alaskan ARCTIC FOX

ARMADILLOS in the sand
  Same as Tonka toys
Both of them unbreakable

B

The BADGER was a real pest
He'd dig up my yard
Over and over again

There once was a BALD EAGLE
Whose name was Harry
But he never got the joke

The BARRACUDA was fast
But I saw him first
In the sea off Norman's Cay

The BAT knew where he was at
No one else did, though,
His black caves were bright as day

Clemmie lived three doors down
Queen of all she saw
Los Robles' sweetest BEAGLE

Some karmas can't be changed
Yet some rivers can
A BEAVER is all it takes

The unhappy BEAR sat up
The zookeeper knew
Some black grapes would make him smile

Ignore the laws of physics
They say BEES can't fly
Wonder what else can't be done

The BEETLE hummed a tune
A simple solo
His band of four had split up

It's not a shiny black bead
With a red hourglass
It's a BLACK WIDOW SPIDER

Scrawny BLUE JAYS in a row
New feathers, wide beaks
Back and forth tired parents

The BLUE RINGED OCTOPUS
Cool enough to touch
But not enough to die for

Sliding down King Cotton's slopes
The South was saved
Hail, the mighty BOLL WEEVIL

Once, from atop western bluffs
Brown rivers of mud?
No, great herds of BUFFALO

Lying face down in the grass
  A different world
Full of BUGS and mysteries

Red flowers wave in the wind
  Cold BUTTERFLIES come
Do you think they feel the heat?

C

Boiling winds churn heat and dust
My CAMEL plods on
In two days, an oasis

The little CANARY sings
Hard work for soft coal
The shift done, men join the song

CARDINALS and Valentines
It's that time of year
Both declare love in their hearts

A CAT's sense of night and day
Is never 12 hours
Naps-to-order on demand

I touch the CATERPILLAR
He keeps on eating—
He has plans for Mexico

CHAMELEONS in some chamois
Should be a title
For John D. McDonald's book

The CHEETAH sat very still
Except for his tail
It was waving like a flag

Cross the road or maybe not
  CHICKENS' dilemma
Will it make a difference?

End of day, serene and still
  A whoosh and chatter
CHIMNEY SWIFTS have returned

Balls, soirees, the opera
  'Must be seen' dates on
A CHINCHILLA's calendar

Dawn on CHINCOTEAGUE Island
  Conquistador ghosts
Race their PONIES on the shore

CHIPMUNKS' agents never call
  No more movie parts
All they want are avatars

A CLAM had a secret wish,
  To be an oyster
His pearls stayed grains of sand

A COCKROACH hides in the night
  Avoiding danger
Did he talk to dinosaurs?

Red and black, a friend of Jack
  Or red and yellow?
The CORAL SNAKE glides away

Wet CORMORANTS on a fence
  Arms stretched out wide
They believe they are scarecrows

4 AM and I must go
  Cold floors tempt me stay
I've impatient COWS to milk

In the hills above my camp
  Singing COYOTES
Sound like cowboys on the trail

To be a CRAB must be fun
  Never worrying
Every tide brings dinner

Though sometimes known as crawdads,
  CRAWFISH reign supreme
Bayou country royalty

CRICKETS can’t send telegrams
  ‘Click, click’—Morse code ‘M’
It’s the only one they know

Half hidden in the tall grass,
  A beaded bracelet
“Finders keepers,” said the CROW

D

As delicate as old lace
  The DAMSELFLY rests
I watch her without breathing

Two DEER were in Mom's garden
  Must have been hungry
Only thing left were footprints

Glass-like DIATOMS float by
  In my microscope
Designs of art and function

"Did you see the DIK DIK's hat?
  Think it's too frou-frou?"
"No. I think it's just so-so."

Happy is the lonely DOG
  Who finds his master
Without knowing his full name

Children know what DOLPHINS love
  Tossing fish to them
Gets joyful gurgling "Thank Yous."

The DONKEY's cross on his back
  Documented fact.
Was it from a miracle?

The DORMOUSE wanted to sleep
  Hibernation time
Let the others rise and shine

A DOVE's black eye watches me
  On guard and ready
One false move and she'll be gone

The troubadours all were wrong
  Their songs should have said
St. George and the DRAGONFLY

New DUCK Crossing signs are up
  Children count and shout
"Eight, nine!" babies have been seen

DUST BUNNIES multiply fast
  Shades of gray and beige
You would think they were for real

E

EARTHWORMS wiggle in my pail
  Nervous little things
I swing my pole, laugh, and run

Mid-Atlantic phone troubles
  Static on the line
ELECTRIC EELS calling home

Does the old EGRET regret
  Life not in the South?
Snowy lands were all he knew

Walking away quietly
  Not a sound was heard
Were they phantom ELEPHANTS?

Once again the ELK was late
  Had no idea
Migrations wait on no one

Don't try to race an EMU
  A fool's silly dream
You will never, ever, win

F

The FALCON hesitated
  Her eyes straight ahead,
She fell from the sky like rain

Solenopsis invicta
  Something to avoid
Known to science as FIRE ANTS

Seven FIREFLIES in a jar
  How incredible–
Instant meadows in my room

Schools of FISH everywhere
  For the young and old
Lesson 1: Avoid the sharks

See those FLAMINGOS tango
  Dance competitions
Have really gone to the birds

A FLEA in the flue, how droll
  A perfect poem
Too classic to be redone

A little boy's shirt pocket
  For FLYING SQUIRRELS
Second best to Mother's nest

A bureaucrat's dream office
  Quick brown FOXES type
Clerks gossip and paint their nails

G

Mama GATOR guards her nest
  With an evil stare
Missing nothing…Not a thing

The GAZELLE's name was Giselle
  Just like a dancer
Had grace of form and movement

My GECKO's like Spiderman
  He can run up walls
Just as high, just as quickly

The GERBILS must be awake
  Soft muffled noises
Plus that constant wretched wheel

All GIRAFFES love Hide-and-Seek
  They can't wait to play
All it takes are foggy days

The advertisement was false
  And so obvious
The GNU knew it wasn't true

A GOAT's choice of what to eat
  Higher or at hand?
The more valued, the better

Swishing their beautiful tails
  GOLDEN PHEASANTS strut
Like little Napoleons

Debate topic for the team
  What's good for the GOOSE
Is not good for the gander

The GOPHER TURTLE's not slow
  Office errand boy
He was faster than the rest

The GORILLA lost his toy
  A magic mirror
It was our face reflected

The GRASSHOPPER picks his teeth
  With his left hind foot
How very convenient

Showers equal GREEN TREE FROGS
  One-note serenades
Love songs as the clouds depart

H

Oh, my, that HAMSTER could dance
  Such a catchy tune
The Internet's favorite

The HAWK circles in the air
  High above my head
I spy thermal underwear

The HEDGEHOG's snout is manic
  Single minded, too
Crazy for the scent of worms

In among gray cypress knees
  One-legged HERONS
Only the moss is moving

Running on the river bed,
  They don't swim at all.
HIPPOS, faster than you'd think

Mr. Ed was real to him
  His own TV HORSE
Too bad life's not black and white

The HYENA's not happy
  No laughing matter
To see his prey run away

I

All I could see were his horns
  Huge, backward curving
And then the IBEX stood up

Mrs. Juana IGUANA
  What a silly name
Still, no one dared tease her

An IMPALA's goal in life
  To be in NASCAR
Thought the Chevys were the best

An American INCHWORM
  Traveled abroad
The road signs were confusing

J

An old JACKAL lies in wait
  Dry twigs bend and snap
His ambush blown, he goes home

The JAGUAR was hot and wet
  Running in the rain
He had been stuck in traffic

For as far as you could see
  JELLYFISH babies
Millions born at the same time

Saharan sands fill the skies
  All tails and long legs
Courting JERBOAS at play

K

KANGAROOS love basketball
Some pro taught them how
Slam dunk jumps were so easy

Like a blessed metronome
The KATYDIDS lull
Fussy children soon to sleep

Perched above flowing streams
Patient KINGFISHERS
Then one dives, then another

The KINKAJOU had to sneeze
A deafening sound
Not a soul could hear for days

The KOALA was in love
Unrequited love
Teddy bears ignored him

Futile bits of wasted bread
No more fish to feed
The KOI pond has been drained

The KOOKABURRA is sad
Exile's not funny
The last boat has left for Oz

I wonder what the KUDU
  Would do if he could
Probably nothing, you know

L

The forest floor seems to move
  Waving flags of grass
LEAF CUTTER ANTS march in step

Who had those dark sultry eyes?
  Dorothy LEMUR
In Bob Hope's Road to Rio

The big LION was moody
  Cubs ignore his pout
His tail, their own jungle gym

2 AM, the lounge was still
  The regulars, gone
The LIZARD stayed for more

The LLAMAS wore pajamas
  Others came in drag
The best Halloween, ever

Hundred LOBSTERS in a line
  Claw-to-tail robots
They had heard old Neptune's call

The sky seems to dip and swirl
  Wheat fields disappear
The air is thick with LOCUSTS

On a dark and lonely lake
  A sad LOON calls out
The echo answers, "I'm here."

The LYNX's ears, antennas
  Twitching side to side
Little mice better worry

M

Hunters huddle in their blind
  The MALLARD sees them
And flies high into the sun

Much like Tai Chi performers
  The MANATEES swim
Slowly, calmly, gracefully

MANTA RAYS are on patrol
  Their black shadows, huge
Vigilantes of the sea

All those MEERKATS are so cute
  Standing on their mounds
An African child's kitty

The sun sure is hot today
  Poor old MILLIPEDE
Every footstep must burn

A special MOLE for certain
  Not blind, he could see
Espionage was his field

Baby MONKEY holds on tight
  Green branches stream past.
His mother's arms, his cradle

Did you hear the MOOSE is loose?
  Cannot get too far
With those antlers six feet wide

Shining through the windowpane
  The candle beckons
The MOTH could get no closer

A MOUSE squeaks in the darkness
  Now I'm wide awake
And another's down the hall

MUREX shells' far best surprise
  Royal purple dye
Their gift to kings and artists

Hot work for sweet molasses
  No carrots for him
Pa's MULE just wants sugar cane

N

NARWHALS have a single tusk
Long, white, and awesome
Mother Nature's Unicorn

The NAUTILUS was a judge
Didn't wear a robe
But he still had his chambers

There are fewer NENES now
Hawaii's state bird
So very rare and unique

O

Oh, OCELOT, what a lot
Of spots you have got
All along your little tail

In an old aquarium
A hole an inch wide
Freedom for an OCTOPUS

The OPOSSUM seemed dead
Danger gone, got up
Not pretending anymore

See the young ORANGUTANS
Playing with their coins
Bet they like the pennies best

ORIOLES are alchemists
Their vivid colors
Transform gray moss homes to gold

Fifty feet up in the air
Two angry OSPREYS
The lineman feints and climbs on

A cook with twelve mouths to feed
Does not need twelve eggs
One OSTRICH's works just fine

Little OTTERS always hear,
  “Slow down…Don’t shove.”
Yet they still go all at once

A hungry OWL hoots all night
  Even in my dreams
Peace at last at break of day

“The width of a planted row
  The width of an OX.”
Said the farmer to his son

P

The PANDA had a problem
  Saw only bamboo
Preferred asparagus

Jewels white, blue, red, and green
  40's haute couture
PANTHER bracelets were the rage

Most PARAKEETS talk a lot
  Get two in a cage
They will twitter all day long

Captain Morgan's old PARROT
  Sure could spin a tale
A swashbuckler to the end

The whole village is on edge
  Safe up in the trees
The PEACOCKS scream of danger

A challenge made on the pier,
  "Who can catch the most?"
"I can," said the PELICAN

The PENGUIN's tux came right off
  A waiter no more
He was soon to be the chef

Grandma told me more than once
Some PETS could be ghosts
'Cause mine sure looks like Granddad

They snuffle in the thick leaves
For a truffle prize
French PIGS, worth their weight in gold

Carrying bags of bird seed
She seeks her moppets,
The Piccadilly PIGEONS

A PLATYPUS's best friend
Has it fur or eggs?
He can't decide whom to choose

Icebergs move in the moonlight
Did I see that right?
No...POLAR BEARS on the prowl

Some shiny PORCUPINE quills
Pioneer mothers'
Favorite knitting needles

The PORPOISE had no purpose
Round and round he swam
Show business was so boring

The PRAYING MANTIS turned
  Eyes focused hard.
The fly…he got religion

One by one the scouts appear
  "Too small." "Too crowded."
House hunting PURPLE MARTINS

Q

Happy childhood memories
  Low tides, QUAHOG CLAMS
Hot chocolate and chowder

Fall…Hunting season's started
  The mother QUAIL runs
All her babies still as stones

A sad denied privilege
  QUEEN BEES never know
Entire lifetimes with a king

The stunning blue green QUETZEL
  A bird for all time
In Mayan hieroglyphs

R

Most Welsh RABBITS don't like cheese
  Makes them cough and choke
So the ones that do are rare

The RACCOON at the crime scene
  Not the guilty thief
Undercover officer

Do you remember Hamelin?
  To enchant a RAT
Melody in D for flute

Did Edgar Allen Poe know
  What the RAVEN did
That would happen, "Nevermore"?

RED VELVET ANT on his hill
  A little Mountie
Same confidence, same color

The Lapp's REINDEER all were lost
  The North Star, hidden
He gave up to wait for day

The RHINO was a poet
  Very sensitive
Not in the least thick-skinned

Signs of Spring: An empty nest
  Blue broken eggshells
It must have been a ROBIN's

My daddy had a ROOSTER
  Didn't live too long
Thought the full moon was the sun

S

They were drawn on Pharaoh's walls
  Once upon a time
The ancient SACRED IBIS

Mermaids long to play Pretend
  SAND DOLLARS for cash
Buy them chests of sunken gold

In true parade formation
  Troops of SANDPIPERS
Sidestep the tide's shifting waves

Fast as jets, SCALLOPS zoom by
  All their vapor trails
A million tiny bubbles

The SCARAB's shiny marble
  His storehouse surprise
Color among the dung balls

Jockey Eddie Arcaro
  A SEAHORSE's dream
Triple Crowns unachieved

Beautiful Monterey Bay
  Deep cold blue waters
Every SEAL's paradise

A SHARK needing some dentures
  A vet's worst nightmare
Something never taught in school

Fur is mostly thick and straight
  Yet some SHEEP have curls
Ha!...So is mine when it's damp

SHRIMP graze on the sandy floor
  Nibbling here and there
Picky gourmet foragers

Fali is a SIAMESE
  No, she's a princess
She says so every day

Some old bookstores have their cliques
  Bookworms are greeted
SILVERFISH are ignored

A blur of blue stripes and brown
  A SKINK dashes by
Hints of sapphires in the grass

My SKUNK adores red roses
  Just like Ferdinand
He'd inhale them all day long

I hear movement in the trees
  Hanging by her toes
The wind rocks the SLOTH to sleep

SNAILS could never hope to be
  Good secret agents
They can't help but leave a trail

Tell a city innocent
  Grab a gunny sack
A-SNIPE hunting we will go

Natives only know his name
  Spots-and-Yellow-Eyes
SNOW LEOPARDS are seldom seen

SOUTH CALEDONIAN CROWS
  Toolmakers, bar none
The smartest birds in the world

He was here, then he was gone
  Hiding in plain sight
The SQUID, the King of Camo

Little oak trees in the yard
  Forgotten acorns
A SQUIRREL's future dinner

The SWAN was aloof and vain
  Too pretty for words,
She would never speak to us

T

Peter Pan, the TADPOLE's role
  Never to grow up
Someone else played Wendy

Daybreak on the Amazon
  On her soft, "All Clear"
A timid TAPIR appears

First they touch and then step back
  Courtship on their minds
TARANTULA minuets

That TASMANIAN DEVIL!
  Did you see his face?
It would scare Beelzebub

TERMITES make one family
  Ten thousand cousins
Pheromone IDs needed

The TERN flew from pole to pole
  Or nearly almost
His sole guide, the stars above

Her cubs fed, the TIGER purrs
  Warmed by the sun
'Cat-endorphins' fill their dreams

Once there was a little TOAD
  Who became a prince
Do you know that fairy tale?

With salty sweat, dust, and luck
  The rock broke apart
A TRILOBITE emerged

No Macy's parades for him
  He's our Grand Marshall
The Albuquerque TURKEY

Ricky's TURTLE couldn't crawl
  Blisters on its toes
Racing liabilities

U

Seeking prey at waterholes
  UNDERTAKER BIRDS
AKA Marabou Storks

V

Neither shrew nor mole is he
  Still, I bet they're kin
To this silky furry VOLE

The VULTURE is as awful
  As anything seen
Ugly is as ugly eats

W

From on high the WALRUS roars
  Fat ladies below
Young males, too close for comfort

The art of Chinese paper
  2000 years old
WASPS were masters of it first

The WEASEL ran low and fast
  Such a commotion
Feathers floated all around

A WHALE's like a ship to me
  Huge from stem to stern
Imagine what the krill thinks

New moon, the night is quiet
  10 times in a row
"WHIP-POOR-WILL" then "WHIP-POOR-WILL"

News bulletin: They're coming!
  Our town is agog
Ten WHOOPING CRANES overhead

Curious but still cautious
  The WOLF looks at me
Have we met somewhere before?

Bravest are the WOLVERINES
  Not that big but fierce
Just the help I'd want in need

To proclaim his small terrain
  A WREN chirps and shrills
It is music to my ears

X

They once were very common
  Now they all are dead
EX-DODOS in museums

Y

Mongolia is so vast
  Do YAKS yak a lot
When they get back together?

First I heard and then I saw
  Dead grass now alive
YELLOW JACKETS on the move

Z

The ZEBRAS pant from the chase
  Another safe day,
Add another stripe for luck

The strong ZEBU pulls his plow
  The rain is stronger
Rows of rice no longer straight

ENVOI

What was once a gift for one is now given to many.
Go with God.

www.ingramcontent.com/pod-product-compliance
Ingram Content Group UK Ltd.
Pitfield, Milton Keynes, MK11 3LW, UK
UKHW062254290726
14090UKWH00017B/676